Sunshine and Rain

A Personal Journey Through Poetry

* * *

By

Janeen M. Thomas

Pathstone Press

Sunshine and Rain – A Personal Journey Through Poetry
By Janeen M. Thomas
Published by Pathstone Press
P.O. Box 476
Copiague, N.Y. 11726
www.pathstonepress.com

This book or parts thereof may not be reproduced in any form, stored in a retrieval system, or transmitted in any form by any means – electronic, mechanical, photocopy, recording, or otherwise – without prior written permission of the publisher, except as provided by United States of America copyright law.

International Standard Book Number:
978-0-9842975-0-4
Printed in the United States of America

This is where I am supposed to
dedicate this book
to someone. Instead, I choose to thank God
for his saving grace, for keeping me
from day to day, for all the
growing pains, and for hope for a better tomorrow.
The best is yet to come.

TABLE OF CONTENTS

INTRODUCTION 1

THE LOVE / HATE RELATE 4

Untitled.. 4

My King... 5

Untitled.. 6

To Know Love... 7

For 8

A Connection.. 11

The Summons and Complaint..........................12

The Glance...15

I Can't Discuss Love....................................16

For _ _ _...18

Disconnect...20

Waiting..23

You..25

Memory..27

Journey..28

For the Moment..31

Crossroads...33

Untitled..35

Last Words...36

Repeat.. 38

What I Need...39

Novelty..40

An Answer... 41

Distant... 43

Unfinished...45

Broken..46

I Hurt...48

Untitled.. 50

No More..51

To My Love..54

Untitled.. 55

Waiting Woman...56

Untitled.. 57

I Wish...58

Untitled.. 59

The Scent.. 60

Typical... 61

RAIN..62

A Poem for Pop-Pop.. 62

The Burden...65

Disillusioned.. 66

Confession of a Schizophrenic.................................68

vi

The Companion..70

Untitled... 72

Sadness.. 73

Uncertain.. 75

Untitled.. 77

Afraid... 79

In Memory of Our Chorus Teacher, Ms. Kaplan......80

They Say..81

Reflection... 83

Apparition.. 84

Fate.. 85

A Prayer.. 86

Almost...87

Hollow...88

Mute.. 90

SUNSHINE..91

Going to Grandma's.............................. 91

Discovery...92

Passages... 94

The Seashore......................................95

Problem Child..................................... 96

Cocoon...97

Ode to My Buick.................................. 98

Raindrops... 100

Seasons...101

Everything Must Change in Life...........................104

Untitled... 106

Christmas.. 107

Battleground.. 108

Untitled... 109

Done... 110

Untitled... 111

After Dusk... 112

Believe In Yourself... 113

Tic Toc..115

End of an Error... 116

Sunshine and Rain.. 119

POEMS LISTED IN CHRONOLOGICAL ORDER........ 120

INTRODUCTION

When I was a student at what was then called the Edmund W. Miles Amityville Junior High School, I immersed myself in the creative writing and poetry clubs headed by a teacher, Mrs. Ettrick, who eventually taught me English literature during the eighth grade. Near the beginning of my ninth grade school year, she gave me a journal and told me to continue writing my poetry in it. I took that to heart, and over the almost twenty years since I received that journal, I continued to write therein. I took the journal to high school where I wrote of meaningless crushes. The journal endured tales of love that mystified me in college, and has continued to endure the pain of loss, happiness and hope.

As my journal nears completion, I thought now was a good time for reflection. So, I have chosen some of my favorite poems for this book and others, while not favorites, are included because they still pull at my

1

heart for one reason or another. Also included are some poems that may reveal more of who I am as a person since I tend to be easily misunderstood, and circumspect, which leaves others unsure of who I am. Like most people, I have experienced a lot of rain in my life. But as a wise person once told me, "without rain, there is no growth." And, as my parents, Nat and Evelyn, my grandmother, Georganna, and Aunt Joyce, always say, "the best is yet to come." I believe that to be true, as my writing has transformed over the years, becoming less dark as I left adolescence to adulthood.

For reasons even unknown to me, I have reached a point of renewal and rejuvenation. I have shaken off the past and am excited for the future. My sincere thanks and appreciation to those of you who peruse these pages. I hope you enjoy the read.

THE LOVE / HATE RELATE

♥ ♥ ♥

Untitled
By Janeen M. Thomas ~ 6.20.95

It grows like a willow

Flowing thru the wind

Fragile as glass

It's nature's perfect blend

Strong as sterling silver

Tender it may be

Love I call it

Between you and me

My King
By Janeen M. Thomas ~ 10.11.09

You quickened my spirit

In quiet trepidation

I trembled inside

Pulsating at rapid rate and

Quivering in thought

I am humbled

Untitled
By Janeen M. Thomas ~ 6.20.95

Twas the perfect night

Seated beneath the starred moonlight

Lovely palms took up the breeze

While his love is what I seized

With sweet breath he called my name

And I did him in the same

Ocean spray did all the cooling

As we finished all our loving

One last kiss and then goodbye

And with one blink, he'd left with the tide…

To Know Love
By Janeen M. Thomas ~ 10.13.09

I would love for someone to love me

I would love to know what it feels like to be safe

I would love to know if I will spend my life with another

I would love for my broken heart to be mended

I would love to know love

For ...
By Janeen M. Thomas ~ 12.19.97

He is the one for me…I think

For his character to me is distinct

But he must love me before my love becomes extinct

How simplistic might I make my plea?

When will it be that he will see

That he is indeed the one for me

Will my desire for him ever be met?

Will he be the father of the sons I beget?

If not, is this a love I will ever forget?

If he is the one, when will God permit?

For I'm desirous to be out of this fit

I don't lie for my feelings are legit…

But I fear this is a one-sided love affair

For this is a statement I'm forced to declare

Oh what a heavy burden for my heart to bare

To love a man who can't understand

To see a man who won't take my hand

To like the man who's in high demand

Whose skin is of onyx, not white or tan

The wait for him I can barely stand

Oh, what a fine gentleman

To be with the man who is fully endowed

The man who walks might tall and proud

To him who I want to make my vows...

Of confident nature and sex appeal

One whose manhood can't be concealed

One who is the real deal

If I could get him whose eyes sparkle

With kinky hair and no s-curl

If only he would call me his girl

Oh, all the things I could do to him

To love a Black man – one of my kin

To be with the man whose mind I can love

To be on the man whose chest I would rub

A love condoned by the God above

To feel his body up and down

My lustful desires unleashed and unbound

Upon him, my king, who should wear a crown

Oh, all the things I would do for him

Filling his soul with sweetness to the rim

For my love for him would never dim

Since he shines among men as a gem

Different in stature from the rest of them

All of this…all of this… for M.

A Connection
By Janeen M. Thomas ~ 9.18.01

Wandering was I through a wooded forest
    Off the path I had fallen
        Daylight blocked by a leafed ceiling

In darkness
    I struggled against an uncertain road
So, through the fog I walked
    Searching for a guide

A cry for help on deaf ears
    Confused and lost . . .
    A hand reached out

Pulled in one direction, I submitted
    Uplifted,
        A ray of hope shown through

Wondering who was my guide
    I discovered my reflection
But in different form, in a different place . . .
    T I M E . . . ahead of me

With awakened eyes
    The surrounding mist I finally realized
    Was . . . you

The Summons and Complaint
By Janeen M. Thomas ~ 7.11.09

To all those who present
To the jerks and the gents
To the men I've met
To the love that went
To the hurts and aches
And to my lost soul mate
Here's my story
No guts no glory
He was short and stocky
Kind of cocky
But here's the part that made it rocky
More downs than ups
Kept me in a rut
So I've been stuck
Waiting for Us
To perpetuate a state
To fabricate a date
To perpetrate a fate
Would all be mistake
Can't you see
There was no you and me
And we were ne'er meant to be
It was hit and miss
A dance and a dis
A kiss that was missed
No joy no bliss
An abyss of remiss

Now here's the twist
He had no balls
He had no gall
He only stalled
He never called
And, waiting for him
Was my pitfall
A look a glare
A vacant stare
It was unfair
To my despair
I wanted to try
I wanted to cry
I wanted to die
I wanted to lie…
Next to you
Til things ensued
But you never stepped up
You had no guts
You totally sucked
You became such a punk
Now, you're a joke
A bloke for other folks
You're not a real man
You deserve that raggedy Ann
And you'll see
She's no me
So good luck with that
And that's a fact
I'm not a hater; just,

See you later
This is my final act
I don't want you back
I decree and declare
You're out of my hair
I break the curse
I put me first
I'll do my thing
And fling the do
Because I'm so much
Better off without you

The Glance
By Janeen M. Thomas ~ 4.20.93

Passing by you that summer day, I stole an innocent
glance at your handsome face

Your burning eyes, your muscular body, I couldn't
stand it anymore and my head I turned with great
haste

It was just one innocent glance – a moment in time –
and there you stole my heart

Your eyes made quick love to mine and then you
disappeared – this romance was wrong – right from
the start

A hungry passion felt deep in my bosom was
something I could not ignore

Because there I stood perspiring and lusting for you
even more

But I uttered not one word and let you go knowing
that this love was not true

For it was just a glance – one harmless look – that
happened to be shared between me and you

I Can't Discuss Love
By Janeen M. Thomas ~ 1.22.98

Don't ask me about love

Why?

Because the subject makes a tremendous, yet very

steady pain swell up deep within my bosom . . .

I hurt, or, rather, the subject hurts me

I daren't think on it

So I can't discuss love

I can't discuss how I feel when . . .

When always dissed by this one and that one

That my love is consistently unrequited

That no one will love me back

Or, that another Valentine's Day approaches and there

is no one there . . . for me

Excuse me, ummm, but do you know what that feels

like?

Uh, no . . . I'm sure you don't

So, I can't discuss love . . . with you

The subject of love makes me dwell on an emptiness
That lives within making daily contribution
To my seemingly eternal emptiness
Of loves that should've, could've
But would not

Not only of loves, but likes, companions and friends
as well
All gone . . .
The pain . . . my pain growing . . . growing
I can not stay . . . here
I can not discuss love

Look what it's doing to me, or rather
The damage for want of it . . .
Something I yearn for most sincerely in my life
A love . . . A special one
One for me
So, don't you see
Why I can't discuss love

For _ _ _

By Janeen M. Thomas ~ 12.19.04

I'm scared to let you hold my heart in your hands for I
wonder what you will do with it
For my heart is a fragile thing

Beautiful it is to find love wherever it may be and
with whomever might be your companion

How lonely it is to journey on the path which is life in
solitude

I thank God for his mercy in giving me a second
chance in hope … in love … in life

Not that I yet bask in ignorant bliss of happiness, but
that I've found someone who has penetrated me . . .
        My soul . . . my mind . . . my heart

The icy barrier which has long guarded my heart since
the yester years slowly fading . . . fading . . . almost
gone

My thoughts turn to a subtle burning within – a
yearning not of lust but in respect and want for the
man who has gazed within my soul and found a
beautiful thing

Mourning no longer in the past . . .
Now looking to the future

No longer satisfied to surround myself with the being that I can live with, but finally, the desire has now overcome me to fight to be with the one I can't live without . . .

That is love.

Disconnect
By Janeen M. Thomas ~ 5.1.96

I have a love, but my love cometh not

Escaping reach within my grasp, I weep

Loving him as I did so

How wrong I was

My love repelled, rejected

Me . . . dejected

Alone, I wait

Unsure if this sweet prince is to be mine

He leaves . . .

       Me in grief

I am not to follow

Should I try?

My love . . . our love . . . his love

Unconnected, Apart

       Though he stole my heart

Waiting, I in want of a chance

Please help me

Assuage my soul

He knows me not

Forgotten I

My existence

Fading away . . . away

Today I ask

Can you love me back

Time no object

Patience my virtue

For you I'll do all

Listless breath that glances my way

Not touching, though

A mere stare, a touch, afraid

That his love would be rejected

He dejected . . .

     By me

Fear doth ease none

Manifested barrier fostered by it

He stops

     Questions . . . unsure

No response

A dead pulse

Love dies

Together pained

Separated

Apart

Waiting

By Janeen M. Thomas ~ 3.18.94

Do you know how much I love you

I can only guess

Relishing the moments we share

In my thoughts, my dreams

On my mind all the time

I want to give my all to you

Sweet inspiration

Oh dangerous desire

How did I fall in love with you

Was it those stunning eyebrows

Or that chiseled chin

Possibly that perfect smile you greeted me with

No words may define how much I love you

The subtle nervousness I feel in your presence

With hair on end I hesitate a kiss

Read my mind O treasured one

Bring me into your world

The time we've left is but so short

Deny me not the foreplay we could have

I'm more than promiscuity itself

The games we could create – beyond imagination

Seduce me my love

I'll give you all you want

And when we're through

You'll regret it not

You
By Janeen M. Thomas ~ 11.6.95

I've got so much love to give you

Why won't you come to me

I've wanted you from day one

Haven't you recognized it from the start

This emptiness I feel

Is only one you can fill up

My heart . . . alone

All I want is that you love me

To feel your powerful gaze

Commanding my spirit on a warm summer day

To have your muscular arms

Enclose my fragile body

To see your passionate breath

Amidst the morning frost

To hold your course hand

Along a path paved by autumn leaves tossed

To kiss you by a waterfall

While being showered by the gentle mist

To enjoy our silence together

While our hearts beat in sync

O, what I shall love to do with you

What I'd love to do for you

The depths my love would reach for you

If . . . you'll have me

My virgin soul

Waiting to be violated by you

. . . And only you

Forever

My love will last

Just come

And, it will be yours

Memory
By Janeen M. Thomas ~ 8.7.93

A memory of you
  Clear as the midnight sky
A red robin sings
  Songs of love long lost
Where did time go?
As if it were yesterday
  You held me in your arms
You visited me not
  And left the phone undialed
Out of my mind I cast
  Your lingering soul as the
Memory of you drowns in my
  Untamed sea of forgetfulness

Journey
By Janeen M. Thomas ~ 5.18.96

Alone

Him not there
Me
Standing afar
Wanting him
Unable to grasp
Fading
Shadows of me there

Where is he?

Heart conquered
Trapped
Guessing
The destination of his love
Unclear
To me
No answer
To my call

O gentle touch
Read my pulse
Grab my hand
Hold my heart
Fear not

Love true?
Sure as light means day
Night means dark
On this simple passion
Worn over time

Wrong undone
Yet no right
The plight unfinished
Two lovers
Apart

Afraid

She not there
Gone
Away from he
Or he from her
Unsure

Missing his timid way
That gentle hand
Calm eyes on her
Uncertain the future

May paralleled paths cross?

One day if fate permits
Then love will live
Happiness will be

Eternal
With hearts intertwined
Inseparable
. . . he and she
Together . . .
    In love

For the Moment
By Janeen M. Thomas ~ 7.10.96

By his side I stand
And him by me

Where?

I know not
But together we are
Happy
Free
In love

As I look into eyes
Shining like crystal
Under moonlit skies
I sigh

My small hand inside his

Warmth

As I could ask for nothing

Of him

Seeking more

For moments like this

I live

Him and I

Kiss

Crossroads
By Janeen M. Thomas ~ 5.18.96

Why was he there?

Why did he come?

A self-invited guest

Why was she there?

Why did she greet? . . . he

An eager host . . . she

Her attentiveness

His absentminded way

Him aloof to her

Or was he?

Her attention towards him

Or was she?

Disguised jealousy on both sides

As he could care not if she was with another

As she should care not when he was with another

Or did they?

Sorrow hidden when he slept with another

Anger exposed when she kissed another

Words unspoken

Emotions suppressed

Formal affections delivered

Only friends at best

Dialogue thru eyes

Shared moments and shy glances

A simple goodbye at last

Feelings failed to be expressed

Truth remaining unknown

Their time unfinished

Anticipation of the future . . .

Until the next crossroad

Untitled
By Janeen M. Thomas ~ 9.19.01

I loved over and over

I thought the well had finally run dry

But you replenished me

I thought I only knew you in my dreams

Somehow you entered my reality

I'm glad you're here

Finally, my heart's in sync with another

No more do I have to explain my idiosyncrasies

You understand or you have them

The strange code we speak is us

Last Words
By Janeen M. Thomas ~ 1.23.94

Save Me…
   Caress Me…
      Love Me…
Hold Me Tightly.

Don't You Ever Leave Me,
I Love You…
   I Need You…
      I Want You…
Don't You Ever Go.

Forever in my heart –
You'll be there
   I'll hold you.

Dry my tearful eyes…
   I'll miss you –
Calm my fearful body…
   I'll kiss you.

My shuddering soul –
   Lonely…
Shield Me
Protection is your name.

Soothe Me…
　Feel Me…
　　Free Me…

Your body on mine…
One more time.

Repeat
By Janeen M. Thomas ~ 3.14.97

I was so stupid

I don't know why I let this one inside my head

What's worse is that I let him stay there

I allowed my hopes to get up

Of course, he was ignorant to the fact he'd done all

this for me

Little did he know how much he'd lighted up my life

Yet, he left me glowing inside

I felt the flame burning

And he blew the candle out

Now I am disappointed

My hopes have dissipated

I know the truth now

I recognize that he does not care about me

Simply, I am an expendable friend

Here I am now, in the waste can

Will someone help me out?

What I Need
By Janeen M. Thomas ~ 12.22.97

I need a man with some dignity

A man who knows how to comfort me

A man who pays his bills on time

A man who dislikes beer for wine

A man who wears real tailored suits

A man that will give other women the boot

A man that will treat me like a queen

A man who won't be nasty or mean

A man who speaks so properly

Without using any profanity

A man who will give me flowers

One whose kisses don't grow sour

A man that will place me on a pedestal

A man to whom I'm his favorite jewel

A man who shows he cares in action not words

A man to whom loving is not absurd

I need this kind of man, yes I do

And I hope this kind of man is in search of me, too

Novelty

By Janeen M. Thomas ~ 3.16.94

Friendly voyage
A new experience
Unheard pleasures
Wanting more
A gentle push
It doesn't hurt
Welcome pressure
Needing more
A hesitating sigh
Slow perspiration
Increased rhythm
OHHHhhh...gasm
Relaxing the pace
Exhaling
Bodies intertwined
Release

An Answer?
By Janeen M. Thomas 10.3.96

It is he who I wait for

I know him now

Had I been asked of whom it was

A mere two months ago, I would not have known

But as I dreamt he came to me

Trying to make a break from my imagination to my

reality

But now that it's been revealed

I know now what to do

My heart aches to see him

For now I wonder how long it shall take

When will it be that we will share a warm embrace

Oh, now I know his name

I want him so . . .

I miss him . . .

Oh . . . for absence has made my heart grow fonder

And confidence has grown that we should be together

With no other have I felt such certainty . . .

That he is the one for me

I pray to God that our love will become true

But only time will tell . . .

And so it is he that I wait for

Distant
By Janeen M. Thomas ~ 3.11.94

I wouldn't know it if love slapped me in the face
I live a solitary life and feel disgraced
He lied to me – that's my hunch
I didn't know love could hurt so much
My heart aches – have mercy on me
Emotional pain and agony
Perhaps staying single is the key
It's not like I'm eager to hit the sack
It's just that there's no one to love or love me back
All these years and not one kiss
No affectionate hug or love's innocent bliss
Inadequacy is what I feel
I'm just a girl dying to be held
Don't the guys know, can't they tell
Unloved, undesired, that's how I'm treated
Too many tears wasted – defeated
How much longer am I to bare the pain
No hope or healing balm – insanity is my claim

All I want is love's embrace
And to forever escape this solitary state

Unfinished

By Janeen M. Thomas ~ 10.3.96

Here I sit again
Taking to my pen
I sit in reflection
Upon some contemplation

I know I did wrong!

I should have loved him
I could have loved him
And yet I would not

Now I sit alone
        In the discomfort zone
My heart has turned to stone
My actions I can not condone

But was it all my fault?

Broken
By Janeen M. Thomas ~ 11.10.96

I am so afraid of tomorrow

I wish not to see his face

What shall I do?

What will he say?

To me he must become the faintest memory

Of the past, our past?

I know not even what to call it

A casual thing

A slight romance

Meaningless

A waste of time

And now . . .

I hurt

I wanted him

I liked him

And I may never have him

How cruel! Unfair! Unjust!

I deserve better and yet I receive it not

I despair . . .

I Hurt
By Janeen M. Thomas ~ 11.10.96

I can not tell you why I hurt so bad
Or why it feels like my heart is bleeding
Or why my eyes are filled with tears

All I know is that I've taken to the pen and paper so
that some of my hurt might go away
I can not say if it is working
I still have not mustered the strength to face the world
What I know is that I hate feeling this way

Strangely enough, it was only 'lil more than a month
ago where I was writing here trying to get over
someone else
I had thought it would be forever 'til I felt this way
again
Guess I was wrong

Pained I am, though, over another case of "like"

And so I don't know why I hurt so badly

Maybe it was my desperate hope that this "like" might

miraculously turn into "love"

But I am wrong . . . wronged again

And so I hurt

Untitled
By Janeen M. Thomas ~ 2.4.95

Oh strangest passion, greatest desire, most hunted
one,
I search for you
One lesson I did learn nearly o'er year's time,
Learned, did I, that you could never be mine.
Why?
As if my longing and lusting meant nothing
Gone unnoticed, it faded away
Lost
Mirror of tears where my image lay may soothe no
broker heart
I know you don't care
Teased, you stole the one thing I hunger most
O hunted one, it's a most dangerous game you play
Greatest desire, why leave me in such dismay
Strangest passion, I'll never stop my search for you
I know your name – your name is Love

No More

By Janeen M. Thomas ~ 12.22.97

No more men who go to jail

No more men who need my bail

No more men with no money

No more men who pretend to love me

No more men with golden teeth

No more men who act like thieves

No more men with Beamers and Benz's

No more men who run up expenses

No more men who mistreat ladies

No more men who just make babies

No more men who speak rap lyrics

No more with the same old rhetoric

No more men who don't have a job

No more men who run with the mob

No more men who disrespect me

No more men with profanity

No more men who don't have a car

No more men who live in a bar

No more men who won't use a phone

No more men still livin' at home

No more men who keep it on the down low

No more who act like my friend, then foe

No more men who push me to the side

No more men who call me for a ride

No more men with baggy jeans

No more with pants stretched at the seams

No more men with dirty fingernails

No more men who tell tall tales

No more men who don't hold the door

No more men who are dirt cheap or poor

No more men with wrinkled clothes

No more men who cheat with ho's

No more men who work at Hess

No more men with a Smith and Wess

No more men who are lazy bums

No more men who are just plain dumb

No more men who display ignorance

No more men who need an allowance

No more men who smoke on weed

No more men persistently in need

I just need a man with some integrity

To My Love
By Janeen M. Thomas ~ 3.18.94

I adore you

I love the way you smile

Your handsome face against the sunshine

Tender lips against mine

I must have you

My love, my joy, my happiness

Sweetheart of mine

Thinking of you while you're away

Watching the seconds pass

Waiting for your return

New passions felt

My love I want your more

Needing that firm body

Upon my womanly self

Caressing me I relish your scent

Until next time my sweet prince

Promising our next encounter

Will outdo the last

Untitled

By Janeen M. Thomas ~ 2.6.95

I long for what was once there
In my heart, my dreams, thoughts, and breath...
It lies
One eternal moment, and my soul escaped into
yours...
And there it stays
To go back in time?
To savor that moment
Just to stay there
But we can't
I wander now
Not in a world of misery
-- One of longing
A passion not meant to be
An empty void which only you can fill
Weeping willow is the woman I've become
A graceful yawn from one time into another
Awakened...you are there

Waiting Woman
By Janeen M. Thomas ~ 2.6.95

There is a silence that waits
Isolation is her fate
A man did her wrong
The blues are her song
There was another she in the way
So she told him he could no longer stay
Now, there is a silence that waits
Tonight there is no date
He called to apologize
And she pushed him to the side
The woman's heart was maimed
She does not care to hear his name
So, there is a silence that waits
A solitary radio curses the silence not
But she takes pride in what she's got
Another will come to love her better
He'll be there and won't upset her
A fine man to be her final mate
Yes, there is another who waits

Untitled
By Janeen M. Thomas ~ 6.20.95

I dreamt of my love
>But he I ne'er saw

Visiting in my sleep
>Vanishing by my wake

A phantom romance
>A black stallion at that

The tangible I sought
>Appearance he escaped

For want of he
>Agony was my fate

A date with my love
>I could never make

So until we meet
>My dreams I await

I Wish

By Janeen M. Thomas ~ 3.20.95

I wish upon a star
I was told my dreams would come true
They don't
LIES!
I wish for my love
He is not here
I long for him
My broken heart greatly pained
I cry
Where is my love?
That's the question I ask
The stars assuage me not
My love is not there
Alone
Why must I weep?
A soul as kind as mine has found no mate
Hoping my love will come one day
I wait…

Untitled
By Janeen M. Thomas ~ 3.10.98

O'er the hills and

    Valleys I go

Wandering and

      Looking

   Wanting

Him so . . . this is the

Man I want

   In my dreams

   In my breath daily

Strong arms around me

Surrounding my very

   Essence ... This is love

The Scent
By Janeen M. Thomas ~ 10.2009

I caught the scent of a man

One with wisdom in his eyes

And thoughtful stance

I looked at him

He wasn't mine

Typical
By Janeen M. Thomas ~ 7.11.09

I wanted to write this ballad

To tell you how much I've had it

But I can't

Because my heart has softened

I think of you often

And so I'm left with a

Heart that swells when I think of you and

Wondering if my feelings lie or are they true and

Missing you daily because that's my frailty and

Wanting you to know that I'm over it all

And so on you I call to try again

RAIN

☔ ☔ ☔

A Poem for Pop-Pop
By Janeen M. Thomas ~ 02.02.02

It is hard to study while my heart is grieving
    This cancer lurking in my Pop-Pop was so
    deceiving

I keep thinking about his funeral and how I will feel
    Shall I sob uncontrollably or the true feelings
    might I conceal

Twas just early December that my dear grandfather
was diagnosed
    That's when doctors discovered to pancreatic
    cancer he was a host

When I heard the devastating news, I nearly passed
out
    For he didn't deserve this – of that I have no
    doubt

My heart broken, shattered, in pieces
    To God I prayed for His undying love never
    ceases

For strength I prayed to be able to endure the anguish
of loss
    To be able to accept God's will no matter the
    cost

Many happy memories have I
    They make it a little easier to say goodbye

He was the best grandfather a kid could ever hope for
    So easy to love, cherish, and adore

Of him I was quite fond
    And, we shared a birthday – a special bond

Pop-Pop, I can't imagine tomorrow without you
    On September 13th, what will I do?

But in my heart, I will always hold you close
    I could never forget someone so intelligent,
    funny and verbose

How I long to hear you tell me one more story
    How sad I am you won't be there the day I
    marry

I see you through a child's eye as I write this simple
poem
    Although I'm an adult now, that's where my
    feelings stem

It's hard to be mature and strong throughout this
        When I feel like the floor's been ripped from
        beneath my feet and I'm falling into an abyss

But I know you're in a better place where you feel no
more pain
        Cause to see you in such distress was quite a
        strain

Pop-Pop, I prayed God would give you peace to end
the suffering and misery
        In the meantime, you were a man who faced
        death with much dignity

I tried not to cry in front of you
        But truly that was one of the hardest things to
        do

Now, God has brought you home, and you are finally
free
        Pop-Pop, I miss you, but now you are an angel
        watching over me.

The Burden
By Janeen M. Thomas ~ 8.14.90

I have a problem…a burden
   The cause, well, is uncertain

This burden I have brings sorrow and grief
   The thing that took my joy was but a thief

My heart is suffering so much pain
   How much longer will this burden remain

I feel like I have no identity and own no name
   This burden on me plays an unfair game

I know I must even up the score
   For this burden is one I can't ignore

This wretched burden that undermines my self-worth
I wait in sweet anticipation of my rebirth

Disillusioned
By Janeen M. Thomas ~ 3.11.94

I'm so lonely

God, please help me

I don't want to live anymore

It hurts so much

I can't go on

No one there for me in my darkest hours

I'm all alone

No peace

Internal turmoil

No solution

No end

Alienated

In my closet

On my bed

No escape

No end

Isolated

In my heart

In my mind

No love

My soul

Unloved

Confined, Imprisoned

Backed in a Corner

Vulnerable

Insecure

Please protect me...

Inside

I cry

Confession of a Schizophrenic

By Janeen M. Thomas ~ 12.29.92

I'm alone, desperate, feeling my way in the darkness

I'm confused, inferior, angry and so I confess

I swear I fervently try to withhold my tears

But they fall off my cheeks anyway

I lie on my bed trying to escape from the world

Almost finding comfort in night versus day

But I'm scared in the darkness cause that's where I'm lonely most

Yet it shelters, protects and hides me…night is a controversial host

What to do? Where to go? I can't live like this forever

I'm ready to release these burdens and feel as light as a feather

I wish it wasn't like this – I wish this sorry situation could have been prevented

But this is the way life is with a broken heart that can never be mended

I hope and pray my circumstances improve this minute

For this is the confession of a schizophrenic

The Companion
By Janeen M. Thomas ~ 9.19.91

I don't wish to remember yesterday's hurts

For they were too great engulfing me like quicksand

The more I struggled, the lower I sank

      Into the pit of hopelessness

Misery was my companion and he knew me well

Every day he visited me from dawn til dusk

Once I gave him the key to my heart, he refused to

part

      Loving my insides he did over and over

In cold, harsh darkness I died while he lived

Vacant eyes looking at other's eyes who did not see

mine

But misery was my constant companion who

commanded my cries

Or maybe I wasn't there

A phantom image I was

Walking and yet not walking

Talking and yet not talking

Lonely and yet not alone

Life was moving – I stood still

Misery dominated my frozen frown

I, the pawn, would follow

Then I realized I was inside myself

I murdered Misery, a newborn creature was rebirthed

The veil lifted, I was free

This new beginning was my destiny

Untitled
By Janeen M. Thomas ~ 11.1990

Look at me
I'm healthy yet unwell
My smile displays happiness but sadness you cannot
tell
I joke. I laugh...I frown. I cry.
Love and sympathy is something I should not be
denied

Sadness
By Janeen M. Thomas ~ 12.5.90

I feel alone and backed in a cage
   I am left in a furious rage

I don't understand others and others don't understand
my needs
I'm crying in my lonely bed with no one there to sit
and hold me

Happiness once glowing warm in my heart was
snatched away
I walk the long, barren roads with no one to talk to
day after day

My life is going in the wrong direction – down
I just can't free myself from this situation – bound

Dark shadows have totally covered my dreams of
hope
Depression once made me think of succumbing to
knotted rope

Even though I'm on the outside of a window looking
in
I'm confident that joy is something I will one day win

Uncertain

By Janeen M. Thomas ~ 10.30.92

I'm so afraid, timid – my heart full of fear

Why am I treated with disgust though I'm so sincere

I try so hard just to gain their approval and still not
respected

I share with them, display my feelings and left
emotionally naked

I'm so cold, heartless, empty inside

I shed tears in disgrace – I've lost my pride

I've let them in, described my hurt, searched for
comfort

I was shunned, forced to leave, feeling
crushed...down with the dirt

It seems my good intentions were twisted into evil

I didn't deserve this – their actions like poison – lethal

Anger, hostility, and ignorance won't help at all

I guess I've got to stick it out winter to fall

I've run out of options – no one to turn to

I need to escape and feel renewed

I need to gain a sense of who I am

Difficult it is when feeling eternally damned

I'm still so sad and eternally weep

I hurt inside – this wound runs deep

I'm so vulnerable and sensitive too

I sit here lonely feeling blue

I wonder and ponder if they make fun of me

Is my appearance amusing? Do I dress that
fashionably

I hate them all and frown my face

Fear has my heart beat at rapid pace

I want to run away and find liberty

Then and only then will I finally be free

Untitled
By Janeen M. Thomas ~ 2.15.91

Depression as always has entered my heart again

I can't remember where happiness ever began

My fragile heart of hope was completely shattered

Nothing can fix it, not even laughter

I was happy, I was glad

I became angry...very sad

Where do the rays of happiness and hope lie

If someone doesn't place me on the right path I might die

Too exhausted from these emotional roller coaster rides

I'm lonely so lonely and no one is on my side

Today I'm totally and emotionally drained
My face filled with grief – permanently pained

My life is almost over and I near the end of the line
I all but accept that happiness will never be mine

Constant scary shadows hover and draw nigh
But I won't surrender and I will not die

Afraid
By Janeen M. Thomas ~ 11.10.96

I do not understand
I will not . . . I can not
How can this be happening to me?
The heavy heart resting within me wants to beat no
more
How much longer will I last?
Will I?
Can I cry?
They tell me not to
I know I shouldn't
I want to
Stay strong
I don't think I can
Let me give in
But to who or what?
I don't know
I know I have no one
I am afraid

In Memory of Our Chorus Teacher, Ms. Kaplan
By Janeen M. Thomas ~ 11.15.92

Death seems so far away yet its presence always so near

We take tomorrow for granted assuming we'll live to see next year

But we don't know what each new day holds
By God's grace we see how it unfolds

Sadness today – our hearts are filled with sorrow
Gloomy clouds blanket smiles like dark shadows

Tears do not soothe broken hearts in dismay
We must cherish memories and seize the day

Walk tall...stand proud...and sing until our voices are heard

Don't look back and dwell on the past for victory comes in moving forward

Don't mourn the rest of the day, but heal in happy memories

And let us support each other in our time of sorrow for strength comes in unity

They Say...
By Janeen M. Thomas ~ 3.11.94

They say time heals all pain

I don't agree

I've been burdened – oh so long

Probably since before age three

They say it will get better some day

When will that day come?

I've been waiting all my life

And still exactly where I started from

They also say your ship will come in

Maybe I'm at the wrong dock

Passing hours, minutes, seconds

No longer can I stand to watch the clock

They even say to keep your chin up

But there's no choice when so far down

It's so hard to maintain a façade

How can you pretend you're not wearing a frown

Then they say this too shall pass
But what's the point when faced with more gloom
I say that there's really no point to life
Especially when interminably doomed

Reflection

By Janeen M. Thomas ~ 3.16.94

Reflection of myself
I know not who I am
Where do I stand
Intangible is my reflection –
    So far away
Trying to find myself
    Don't know where to start
No soul
No shadow
Alone
My inner being separated
I look for answers
My reflection helps me not
In despair, my reflection
    d i s a p p e a r s
My shadow fades away
Silence

Apparition
By Janeen M. Thomas ~ 3.16.94

They were there, I know they were

Instead, they revealed themselves as false hopes

Dreams I had – great aspirations

Slowly slipped from my grasp

My spirit broken

My heart injured

To no longer wish anymore – a tragedy

Faced with reality

I shudder in fright

Enlightened, apparitions hinder me no more

Fate

By Janeen M. Thomas ~ 3.16.94

Mountainside

I respect thee

Rocky cliffs do challenge me

The thrill of a fall

A temptation, you see

Falling to my death,

To be or not to be

Doom scares me not

I've mastered it to a tee

Wavering on this cliff

My time will come shortly

A simple slip

An unrued step

Meeting the ground

I greet destiny

A Prayer
By Janeen M. Thomas ~ 11.10.96

I can not by any means understand the source of my
sadness
Oh God help me
Please hear the nature of my plea
Here I am left all alone
My soul tormented
As if mine was not a path destined for happiness
For I am greatly despaired
It was not I who sought after Depression
But it is he who stalks me
And alone I cry

Almost
By Janeen M. Thomas ~ 3.16.94

I'm not here to stay

I must flee

Escape to new grounds

Find my niche

Transformation

Freeing my mind

New ideals

Liberty

There's no way I can stay

To find peace

Not adversity

Yes, I will go now

Fleeing my nightmare

Reaching for my dreams

Hollow
By Janeen M. Thomas 3.14.97

What may assuage my broken heart today

Who might whisper consoling words to me

It is a pain that aches and aches and aches

Seeming never to dull

The skies are gray and cloudy

The clouds are crying today

Just as my eyes rained on my cheeks last night

Praying for sleep, it finally came

Only for my morning to greet me with dreadful

emptiness

There is a sour hollowness in my heart

A void that can't be filled

An anguish not to make folly of

My tears are real as is my sadness

Filled with grief, I sigh

Know not I what to do

Feeling like a creature unwanted by others

No affection, no love to give or one who would reciprocate

Nobody cares about me

Conclusion

I am alone

Mute
By Janeen M. Thomas ~ 1.8.94

How desolate thine own page

   It hath no ink

The lined wood doth go unaccompanied

   Ideas unspoken –

      Words unwritten…

Tis a plague of writers block upon thee

SUNSHINE

✳○✳○✳○

Going to Grandma's
By Janeen M. Thomas ~ 2.27.07

There's nothing better than going to Grandma's house.

It's the gathering place where family ties form and bond.

The place for warm meals and sweet treats galore.

A place to play – a place to laugh – a place to live – a place to love...
A place to cry and pray and heal in hugging arms.

With kindness in her eyes and never a harsh word, Grandma is a pillar of strength and the energy of her home.

Her graceful presence has always comforted me as a baby through adulthood.

In my heart of hearts, I always know at Grandma's house, there is love.

Discovery
By Janeen M. Thomas ~ 7.10.96

In a strange and cold place

She shudders

A world unknown

To her

A struggle of survival

Between middle earth and beyond

Where good rivals evil

Two forces pulling upon her

Refuge sought

And none found

With head raised the

Preparation begins

The challenge to arm herself

A need for power amidst

The physical and a yearning

For power within the mind

Two treasures of sole possession

Ones she cherishes

A discovery of her inner strength

And in the beginning of her wisdom

She knows

That she will make it

Passages
By Janeen M. Thomas ~ 7.10.96

A passage in life

A miraculous journey

The road to adulthood and beyond

To trace the path where it all begins

A future discovery of where you will go

Not knowing where it all ends

The phases traveled through

How we safely exit one and enter another

What parts of us mature

And where we remain stoic

To grow gracefully

And how not to age at all

An enigma within itself

Yet time falls upon us all

And we continue to travel on

As mysteries and other jewels

Greet us along the way

Until we discover the end

The Seashore
By Janeen M. Thomas ~ 2.1.93

It really is a beautiful day

It's March, but my heart feels the warmth of a
morning May

Gentle sunny rays of hope caress the peaceful earth

Blue birds sing and twerp in their nests while a
groundhog peeks out of his home for what it's worth

I lay against my picnic blanket and let the sand dance
on my feet

The clouds in the sky play their games too forming
diverse objects in the heat

The ocean breeze lulls me to sleep, it is time to leave
this place

My alarm clock wakes me up and I have a sandy
dandelion on my pillowcase

Problem Child
By Janeen M. Thomas ~ 2.20.93

Dogonit! I've got allergies

Hangin' around cats and dogs make me sneeze

When I get the itchies, Benadryl just won't do

I have to see a doctor and I get the hospital blues

To make matters worse something's wrong with my
stomach

It's constantly bloated and makes me crap the way I
shouldn't

Enough about that – let's talk about my ear

Actually it's fine except I can hardly hear

They say it's minorly clogged and I need Q-tips

But I know the truth – I'll soon be reading lips

Well, these are only minor ailments and I better stop
complaining

I mean it's a wonderful life and I'm glad to be among
the living

Cocoon
By Janeen M. Thomas ~ 6.20.95

In the mirror, it knew what it was

Yet it did not know who it was

Unrecognized the face

The same for body

Unmarked changes had taken place

A new being now in its stead

A creature shy unto itself

Awaiting the unknown

Shying away from its reflection

Cognizant of the shaped shadow

Here to face the world

With unchallenged, yet brave heart

Away it went

Ode to My Buick
By Janeen M. Thomas ~ 2.17.97

This poem is dedicated to my old car

It was a Buick LeSabre

It will be put to rest soon

Because it can travel no further

Now I must bid my car farewell

I must now rely on my own two feet

That old car lasted 13 years

So it is silly now that I should be met with grief

Goodbye now to my white and maroon car

Yesterday you traveled your last mile

I'll miss our long road trips together

But now I must take you to the junk pile

Well, old car, you'll be happier in your final resting

place

My Badmobile will be replaced by another

No more premium gas for you

No longer will I have to shout, "Oh, brother!"

A great car indeed, revered by all

Until you finally stopped and stalled

Although our journey has nearly ended

I wish you would start for one last call

Raindrops

By Janeen M. Thomas ~ 3.20.95

This cloudy morning I awoke to pounding raindrops

above my head

The rhythm matched that of my own heart

Sitting by the windowside, I sighed

A dreary day it was, the sun certainly would not shine

The abandoned woman I am, pools of water falling

off my cheeks matched what had gathered outside

Memories flooding my brain, I thought of what was

I reflect upon the happiness and feel the loneliness

But I must go on

As my face evaporated to dryness

I watched a rainbow slowly form against the sky

As timid as it was, the sun would soon rise

And, I knew, I would, too

Seasons
By Janeen M. Thomas ~ 2.21.93

When I think of summer, I feel the sun cradling my
body and giving me a tan
Silly ocean waters tickle my feet while glistening
upon my back against the sand
Summer's breeze of dawn start the day and awaken
grasshoppers and lady bugs
Its equal breeze of dusk cools the earth bringing out
the fireflies and slimy slugs
Summer – a season where free spirits careless of time
roam around aimlessly
For others, a season where lost individuals sometimes
find their true destiny

When I think of autumn, I see barren trees and prism
leaves lining every street
A more vicious wind races against the land slapping
everyone in the face with its feet

Lonely lily pads float down the river and disappear
beyond the choppy waterfalls
For students, an educational renaissance and sudden
emptiness of malls
A magical time where a shooting star escapes beyond
the horizon without hint or clue
Autumn – a season where the great outdoors offer all
creatures crisper air and minds become more creative
and new

When I think of winter, I sense a peaceful calm that
white snow tends to bring
I get a glimpse of a simple, but crystal like snowflake
whizzing by my face falling...falling...falling
A juvenile snowman stares at everyone riding by
without prejudice
He sees not color but the innocence of the human race
lost in an unknown abyss
Winter – where Jack Frost greets us with harsh winds
and bitter cold

A time when you challenge each new day and see
how it unfolds

When I think of spring, I have been given the pleasure
of remembering an old friend forgotten by time's
quick hands
It is the awakening of bears once in hibernation and
all of nature's children so precious in the land
New flowers pop up, baby birds sprout their wings
and dew drops gently rest on glistening grass
A moonlit night sets the tone for sharing with your
lover magnificent memories from the past
Spring – when toddlers start to walk, a tadpole
becomes a frog, and new fashions highlight a world
that's changing
It's the rebirth of the heart, soul and mind, a totally
new beginning

Everything Must Change in Life
By Janeen M. Thomas ~ 9.28.90

People must change as the leaves must fall
  Hair turns gray as toddlers grow tall
South by southwest the Blue Jay flies
  As the sun must set so the moon may rise
As babies are born people are snatched away
  While a dark night turns into a bright new day
Young naïve minds grow old and wise
  As people continue to foster family ties
With each second that ticks death grows near
  But tomorrow will become today and this is
  something you can't fear
As a pearl escapes a clam a new one forms
With each day we gain an obstacle or triumph over a
storm
As pennies make dimes and dimes make dollars
  kids grow up and become great scholars

And as the world may sleep, America must wake, and in our lives, how things change for us, well, it's a decision that we all must make

Untitled
By Janeen M. Thomas ~ 9.26.90

I'm not sad, but I'm not happy

I'm just observing everything around me

Nothing has changed

Trapped in unsatisfied rage

I go to school and I go home

My mind waits, wanders and roams

In a rut with the same routine

So what does life really mean

Maybe it's not my environment

Maybe it's me

I'll try something new

You just wait and see

This is only the beginning and not the end

I will embrace whatever adventures that life sends

Christmas

By Janeen M. Thomas ~ 12.23.90

Christmas time is a time of giving

A time of happiness and joyful cheering

A time for merry zion songs

Where people do more right than wrong

Parents buy little ones lots of toys

Children give parents tons of joy

Babies stare at festive lights

People try to stay out of fights

But Christmas is more than just a special day

It's also the celebration of Christ's birthday

Christ – the man who saved us all

To accept him is to escape hell's pitfall

Christmas – the most important day of the year

And one week later the New Year is here

So Christmas is a holiday that I certainly adore

Let's keep it safe in our hearts forever more

Battleground
By Janeen M. Thomas ~ 11.10.96

I am kept down

Bounded

One battle after another I fight

The victor, I rest

Yet conquered enemies travail against me

They want something

A part of my self

But it does not belong to them

Though they try to keep me down

They will have to try harder

And I will fight tougher

And I will win

Untitled
By Janeen M. Thomas ~ 3.20.95

When there was time
   I laughed, played, had fun
A smile on my face I was troubled none
   This was when I was young
Living off the comfort of others I lived my life
Worry free, pleasure was mine
Now, that time is gone
Hustle and bustle – comfort is gone
Alone in a burdensome world
Adulthood

Done

By Janeen M. Thomas ~ 10.18.09

Done with sad

Done with mad

Time to get happy

Time to get Glad

Done with wait

And frustrate

The time is now

To make it great

Untitled
By Janeen M. Thomas ~ 3.20.95

Sometimes, it's good

Actually, it can be great

Yesterday, it was terrific

Today it was okay

Tomorrow, well who knows –

What is it?

It can be anything

One never knows what will make you happy

Or very sad

The best thing in the world could happen to you today

Next month you might say the same thing

You never know what life has in store for you

Surprises are wonderful

After Dusk
By Janeen M. Thomas ~ 9.19.01

Anticipation of . . .

    Oh the excitement and joy of tomorrow's today

Commencement of Dreams . . . how wishful

Cherubic skies abound . . . Dawn

Believe In Yourself
By Janeen M. Thomas ~ 10.3.03

I have learned to believe in myself and to trust in God.

I have learned that there are no short cuts to success.

I have learned that just when I have exhausted my internal resources for survival that I always manage to dig a bit deeper and find that light at the end of the tunnel.

I have learned that the journey never ends.

I have learned to pace myself and have found friendship in patience.

I have learned to look forward to broader horizons.

I have learned to look forward to new challenges and not to be afraid of change.

I have learned that I hurt myself the most on the days when I told myself "I can't."

I have learned not to focus on what other people have, but to focus on my own self-improvement.

I have learned that spending time with family and friends is more important that focusing on a new job. I have learned to center myself.

Tic Toc
By Janeen M. Thomas ~ 10.4.09

Now or never
    To be clever
        To pursue a new endeavor

Make it happen
    With some passion
        There's no sense in being passive

Get prepared
    Don't be scared
        Keep taking steps to move forward

Escape the rut
    Don't stay stuck
        Pray for blessings and good luck

So, make the switch
    And make it stick
        Live it now without limit

End of an Error

By Janeen M. Thomas ~ 10.24.09

I pontificate

The great debates

Which led the States

To a new fate...

An overdose of ignorance

Left most ostracized

I will not apologize

It's not my fault we were Palinized

But here I stand

A Black woman

Struggling against

The covert man

Our new president

Is actually of mixed descent

But for reasons I can only guess

I suffer resentment

I think I get blamed
For Obama's fame
For becoming our leader
Isn't that insane

They want to throw stones
Speak LIES! In harsh tones
Watch Fox News just
Moan and groan

The real point is
Bush was no wiz
After eight years
We were tired of missives

Despite his mistakes
I hold no hate
For all the wrongs
We can abate

So there's no point
In divisiveness
We face great problems
And great promises

So, let's get along
Align and stay strong
It's time to unite
Time to move on

Sunshine and Rain

By Janeen M. Thomas ~ 3.20.09

Pardon me, but I can see

It was destiny that led me

Imprisoned then set free

No more anger controlling me

Through depression I misspoke

And the rains of life fostered growth

Time healed my wounds and memories fade

Thank God Almighty for His merciful grace

Now overjoyed to greet each day

There's sunshine in my soul today

Poems Listed In Chronological Order

The Burden...8.14.90

Untitled...9.26.90

Everything Must Change in Life...9.28.90

Untitled...11.1990

Sadness...12.5.90

Christmas...12.23.90

Untitled...2.15.91

The Companion...9.19.91

Uncertain...10.30.92

Our Chorus Teacher, Ms. Kaplan...11. 15.92

Confession of a Schizophrenic...12.29.92

The Seashore...2.1.93

Problem Child...2.20.93

Seasons...2.21.93

The Glance...4.20.93

Memory...8.7.93

Mute...1.8.94

Last Words...1.23.94

Distant...3.11.94

They Say...3.11.94

Disillusioned...3.11.94

Reflection...3.16.94

Almost...3.16.94

Apparition...3.16.94

Fate...3.16.94

Novelty...3.16.94

Waiting...3.18.94

To My Love...3.18.94

Untitled...2.4.95

Waiting Woman...2.6.95

Untitled...2.6.95

I Wish...3.20.95

Untitled...3.20.95

Untitled...3.20.95

Raindrops...3.20.95

Untitled...6.20.95

Cocoon...6.20.95

Untitled...6.20.95

Untitled...6.20.95

Disconnect...5.1.96

Journey...5.18.96

Crossroads...5.18.96

For the Moment...7.10.96

Discovery...7.10.96

Passages...7.10.96

An Answer...10.3.96

Unfinished...10.3.96

You...11.6.96

I Hurt...11.10.96

A Prayer...11.10.96

Battleground...11.10.96

Afraid...11.10.96

Broken...11.10.96

Ode to My Buick...2.17.97

Repeat...3.14.97

Hollow...3.14.97

For ...12.19.97

What I Need...12.22.97

No More...12.22.97

I Can't Discuss Love...1.22.98

Untitled...3.10.98

A Connection...9.18.01

Untitled...9.19.01

After Dusk...9.19.01

A Poem for Pop-Pop...2.2.02

Believe In Yourself...10.3.03

For _ _ _...12.19.04

Going to Grandma's...2.27.07

Sunshine and Rain...3.20.09

The Summons and Complaint...7.11.09

Typical...7.11.09

The Scent...10.2009

Tic Toc...10.4.09

My King...10.11.09

To Know Love...10.13.09

Done...10.18.09

End of an Error...10.24.09

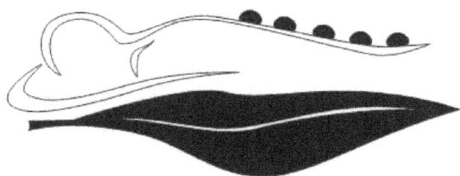

Pathstone Press

About the Author

Janeen M. Thomas was born and raised on Long Island. She is an attorney with a Manhattan based law firm. When not litigating, Ms. Thomas enjoys going to church, reading, writing, biking, swimming and travel.